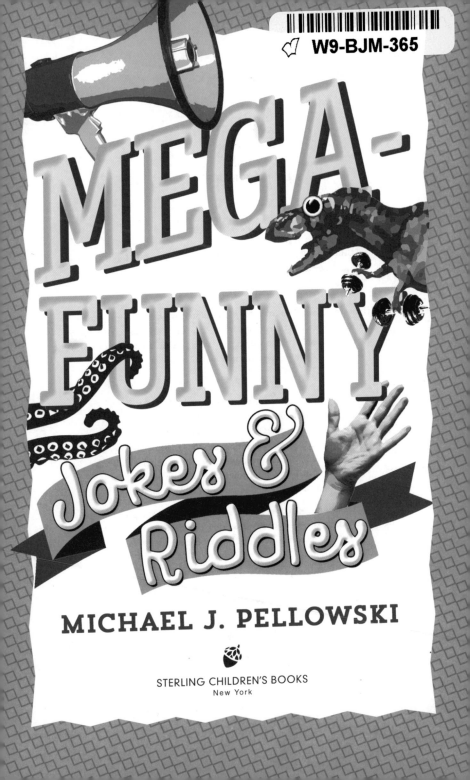

MEGA-FUNNY

Jokes & Riddles

MICHAEL J. PELLOWSKI

STERLING CHILDREN'S BOOKS
New York

To George & Jason Pellowski

STERLING CHILDREN'S BOOKS
New York

An Imprint of Sterling Publishing Co., Inc.
1166 Avenue of the Americas
New York, NY 10036

ISBN 978-1-4549-2255-1

Distributed in Canada by Sterling Publishing Co., Inc.
c/o Canadian Manda Group, 664 Annette Street
Toronto, Ontario, Canada M6S 2C8
Distributed in the United Kingdom by GMC Distribution Services
Castle Place, 166 High Street, Lewes, East Sussex, England BN7 1XU
Distributed in Australia by NewSouth Books
45 Beach Street, Coogee, NSW 2034, Australia

For information about custom editions, special sales, and premium and
corporate purchases, please contact Sterling Special Sales at 800-805-5489 or
specialsales@sterlingpublishing.com.

Manufactured in Canada

Lot #:
2 4 6 8 10 9 7 5 3
07/17

sterlingpublishing.com

Design by Ryan Thomman

Contents

1

Why is bathroom math easy to master? All you have to know is number one and number two.

What did the police officer yell to the bank robber who ran toward the bathroom?
"Hold it!"

What did Mother Star say to Little Star before their long space trip?
"Tinkle, tinkle, Little Star."

What do you get when you put dirt down your pants?

Soiled underwear.

Knock-knock!

Who's there?

Sewer.

Sewer who?

Sewer if she breaks our contract.

What is the smelliest job in the army?

Driving a septic tank.

KOOKY QUESTION

Do vampires refuse to use public batrooms?

Knock-knock!

Who's there?

The odor.

The odor who?

"The odor I get, the worse I smell," said the skunk.

Knock-knock!

> Who's there?

P. Hugh.

> P. Hugh who?

P. Hugh! Somebody smells bad.

What do you say when an owl in a dairy barn has stomach gas?

> "Whoo cut the cheese?"

What do you get when you cross a toilet and a comedian?

> Bathroom humor.

DAFFYNITION

Latrine: an army bathroom where soldiers go to do their duty

Knock-knock!

> Who's there?

Peas.

> Peas who?

Peas close the bathroom door.

What happens if you drop a gush of hot air?

You break wind.

What do you get when you cross
a bathroom and a jogger?

A toilet that runs a lot.

Knock-knock!

Who's there?

Harold.

Harold who?

Harold were you when you stopped wearing diapers?

Which political group did baby Thomas
Jefferson start?

The Democratic Potty.

What kind of restroom is on Mars?

A spaced-outhouse.

Knock-knock!

Who's there?

Avery.

Avery who?

Averyone poops!

KNOCK-KNOCK!

What is the messiest bird in the universe?

The stool pigeon.

Which baby wizard needs toilet training?

Harry Potty.

Why did the toilet need bathroom tissues?

It had a runny nose.

Which space robot looks like a walking outhouse?

R2-DOO-DOO.

What do cowboys call a bathroom?

The Westroom.

KOOKY QUESTION

Do toddler cheerleaders know a good potty cheer?

Knock-knock!

Who's there?

Gwen.

Gwen who?

Gwen ya gotta go . . . ya gotta go!

What happens when a porta potty tips over?

Bathroom breaks.

Where did the #1 football team play the #2 football team?

In the Toilet Bowl.

Which *Star Wars* android always has to go?

C-3P too much.

Which vehicle do you find parked in the garbage restroom?

The dump truck.

DAFFYNITION

Potty chair: a place where parents rear their young children

Knock-knock!

Who's there?

Sy.

Sy who?

Sy-lent but deadly.

What did the toilet water say to the bowl?

"I'm not going around with you anymore."

When is a toddler the most dangerous?

When walking around with a loaded diaper.

Why did the NFL star grab his stomach and groan?

He had pro-pain gas.

GODZILLA: I went to a football game and ate a quarterback. Now I have an upset stomach.

KING KONG: Don't worry. It'll pass.

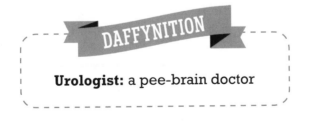

DAFFYNITION

Urologist: a pee-brain doctor

Knock-knock!

Who's there?

Missy.

Missy who?

Missy diapers need to be changed.

What do you get when the crew of an armored vehicle has chili for breakfast, lunch, and dinner?

A tank full of gas.

HA HA HA
HA HA
HA HA

FUN FACT

Dracula's castle has only one master batroom.

2

SUPER SILLY

Knock-knock!

Who's there?

I, Noah.

I, Noah who?

I Noah your secret identity.

QUINN: Is this a Honda motorcycle?

BIKER: No. It's a Harley Quinn.

What lobster is a superhero?

Captain Americlaw.

Which U.S. president was a superhero?

The Incredible Polk.

Where do super villains play organized baseball?

In the Criminal Justice League.

MAN OF STEEL: What's wrong with me, Doc? I have so much energy, it's hard to sleep at night!
DOCTOR: You have iron-rich blood.

Why did Spider-Man hug his waiter?

He found a fly in his soup.

Knock-knock!

Who's there?

Oil change.

Oil change who?

Oil change into my superhero costume in a jiffy.

How did the superhero get a pain in his ribs?

He got a side kick.

PETER: Did you hear the story about the spider that became a superhero?
PARKER: Yes. It's amazing.

Show me a super baker who works out with dumbbells . . . and I'll show you a hero with buns of steel.

Which super heroine walks around aimlessly looking for super villains?

Wander Woman.

Which metropolis does Bat Pinky come from?

Gothumb City.

Knock-knock!

Who's there?

Gus.

Gus who?

Gus who the joke is on, Batman.

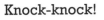

DAFFYNITION

Tin Man: a cheaper version of the super expensive superhero, Iron Man

What did the Invisible Kid say to the other superheroes?

"I'll see you all later, but you won't see me."

BARRY: Did you see the Flash race past us?

LARRY: No. He must have been moving at blinding speed.

Knock-knock!

Who's there?

Hugh Kent.

Hugh Kent who?

Hugh Kent tell my cousin Clark I'm in Metropolis.

What do you get when you give antelopes super powers?

The Gnu Mutants.

GUARD #1: The evil Clock Master just broke out of jail.

GUARD #2: Watch out, world!

Which superhero lives in the forest and has antlers?

Deerdevil.

Who should you call when Super Mariner can't teach his school of fish?

Call a sub mariner to take his place.

What does Aquaman use to call his mermaid girlfriend?

He uses his shell phone.

What does the Jolly Green Giant use to see in the dark?

A Jolly Green Giant Lantern.

KOOKY QUOTE

"I think archery is a nerve-wracking sport," said the arrow master with a quiver.

Knock-knock!

Who's there?

Megan.

Megan who?

Megan this city a safe place to live is not an easy task.

KNOCK-KNOCK!

What did evil Captain Thunder say to Batman?

"Wayne, Wayne, go away. . . . Come again some other day."

STAN: Who is Lieutenant America?
LEE: He used to be Captain America, but he got demoted.

How does the Flash call other superheroes on his cell phone?

He uses the speed dial.

Which superhero lives in a billiard parlor?

Deadpool Shark.

Show me an absentminded superhero . . . and I'll show you a crime fighter who can't remember his secret identity.

A MUTANT BOY AND GIRL WHO'D JUST MET WERE HAVING A DISAGREEMENT.

"I think you're very conceited just because you have super strength," said the girl.

"Humph! Well, do you know what I think?" replied the boy.

"Yes, I do!" snapped the mutant girl. "I can read your mind!"

Knock-knock!

Who's there?

Ozzie.

Ozzie who?

Ozzie a superhero flying overhead.

What happened when Torch Boy began to date Aquagirl?

It started a heat wave.

What is the easiest way to catch the world's fastest superhero?

Use a speed trap.

What is Super Dude's favorite cheer?

"Up, up, and hooray!"

Knock-knock!

Who's there?

Habbit.

Habbit who?

Habbit you read a lot of comic books.

KNOCK-KNOCK!

Knock-knock!

Who's there?

Stanley.

Stanley who?

Stanley, the comic book writer.

Which fish is a superhero?

The Caped Codfish.

Where does Ant-Man spend his vacations?

At his ant's house in the country.

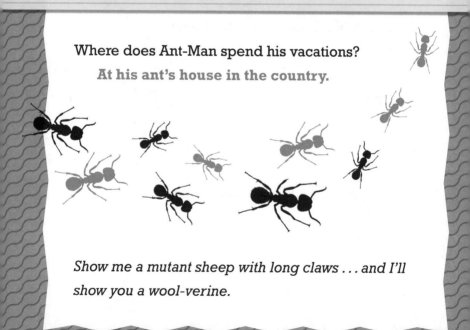

Show me a mutant sheep with long claws . . . and I'll show you a wool-verine.

Knock-knock!

Who's there?

Myron.

Myron who?

Myron across the country at super speed only took twenty minutes.

SUPER GUY: Why is the Flash in court?

SUPER GAL: A cop gave him a speeding ticket.

What do you get when you promote Captain America?

You get a major superhero.

What do you call four superheroes who like to play golf together?

The Fantastic Foursome.

Why did the city of Metropolis hire Super Guy to do its winter snow removal?

They hired him because he has super plowers.

Knock-knock!

Who's there?

Vision.

Vision who?

Vision you a safe trip back to Krypton.

OTHER SUPERHEROES

Captain Golfer—he putts criminals behind bars.

Captain Pugilist—he fights crime while
wearing boxing gloves.

Captain IRS—he makes criminals pay for their
ill-gotten wealth.

Miss Super Ivy—you'll vine her where
trouble is.

Wonder Mom—she has two hands of steel and eyes
in the back of her head.

Why did Flame Girl marry Torch Boy?

Together they were a perfect match.

KOOKY QUESTION

When the Joker goes to a fancy dinner party,
does he get all decked out?

How did the Hobgoblin feel when the Joker was voted Villain of the Year?

He was green with envy.

HA HA HA

Knock-knock!

Who's there?

Disguise.

Disguise who?

Disguise a super villain, not a superhero.

Why can't Superhero Rangers operate during a blackout?

Because the Rangers have no power.

What does the world's fastest superhero use to see at night?

A Flash-light.

Knock-knock!

Who's there?

Mister E.

Mister E who?

Mister E comics are full of suspense.

What does a superhero use to hold his mask in place?

Masking tape.

Knock-knock!
> Who's there?

Hare.
> Hare who?

Hare I come to save the day. Super Bunny's on the way.

What do you get when you cross a pessimist with a PhD and a calendar?
> Dr. Doomsday.

Which mutant superheroes have to study a lot?
> The X-Zams.

What do you get when you give cows super powers?
> *Moo*tant superheroes.

Knock-knock!
> Who's there?

Ida.
> Ida who?

Ida cape, but it blew off while I was flying here.

HA HA HA HA HA

Knock-knock!

Who's there?

Wanda.

Wanda who?

Wanda Woman.

What do you get when you cross a comic book store and a sub shop?

A deli that makes super hero sandwiches.

Knock-knock!

Who's there?

I, Spectre.

I, Spectre who?

I Spectre wondering what my secret identity is.

Knock-knock!

Who's there?

Alma.

Alma who?

Alma friends are superheroes, too.

3

DAFFY DEAD ENDS

Barry: How did the zombie student do in life-science class?

HARRY: It failed.

Who takes care of a swarm of walking undead?

The zombie keeper.

Knock-knock!

Who's there?

I, Zeno.

I, Zeno who?

I Zeno zombies out there, so let's make a run for it.

Then there was the zombie politician who couldn't run for office, so she joined the Cadaverous party.

Why are there no good zombie comedians?

Because zombies are always dead serious.

Knock-knock!

Who's there?

Axel Lee.

Axel Lee who?

Axel Lee, I'm scared to death of zombies.

Why did the zombie quit working?

It was stuck in a dead-end job.

Knock-knock!

Who's there?

Jess Sadie.

Jess Sadie who?

Jess Sadie word and I'll attack those zombies.

Then there was the zombie safecracker who was arrested for breaking into cemetery vaults.

When do you become a zombie carpenter?

After you're dead as a doornail.

Where do you find a zombie mattress?

On a deathbed.

Knock-knock!

Who's there?

Geeno.

Geeno who?

Geeno body told me there are zombies around here.

KNOCK-KNOCK!

Who are Zombie Daffy and Zombie Donald?

They're undead ducks.

FUN FLASH!

The zombie Tin Man refuses to stay buried in his final rusting place.

What branch of the military did the zombie join?

The Funeral Service.

How does a zombie stay in shape?

It joins an undead speed-walking club.

Why did the zombie fail his exam?

He answered every question dead wrong.

Knock-knock!

Who's there?

Hy Otto Bea.

Hy Otto Bea who?

Hy Otto Bea afraid of zombies, but I'm not.

Show me a zombified Sir Lancelot ... and I'll show you the dead of knight.

FUN FLASH!

Then there was the judge who gave a zombie jaywalker a stiff fine.

What does a zombie knight wear?

Dead-body armor.

What do you call zombie corn?

The stalking undead.

What do you call a funny zombie?

The Walking Pun-Dead.

FUN FLASH!

Then there was the zombie who researched his family tree and discovered it was nothing but dead wood.

BORIS: Is it difficult to make the zombie basketball team?

MORRIS: Yes. The competition is very stiff.

Knock-knock!

Who's there?

Alby.

Alby who?

Alby glad when there are no zombies left in this world.

What do you get when you cross a turtle and a zombie?

Slow death.

Why do zombies walk?

They're in no hurry to get where they're going.

How did the zombie halfback escape from the zombie tackler?

It used a stiff arm.

HA HA HA HA HA HA HA HA HA

Knock-knock!

Who's there?

Elsie.

Elsie who?

Elsie if any zombies are lurking outside.

What do zombies drink in the morning?

Burial-ground coffee.

Why did the zombie beauty contestant win the Miss America pageant?

Because she was drop-dead gorgeous.

Why do zombies hate pirates?

Pirates make the undead walk the plank.

What's the dumbest thing a robber can say to a zombie?

"Your money or your life!"

4

ONLINE LAUGHS

Who were the first owners of a computer?
Adam and Eve. They shared the first Apple.

How do you keep debt collectors from entering the estate grounds?
Close the bill gates.

What do you get when you cross a tornado and an online game of global armed conflict?
Whirl of Warcraft.

What did the computer crook
say to the police officer?
 "You can't search me
 without a warrant."

Knock-knock!
 Who's there?
My crow.
 My crow who?
My-crow-soft.

What happened to the dumb computer thief?
 He got locked out and locked up.

KOOKY QUESTION

Do computer quarterback fans have
football passwords?

Knock-knock!
 Who's there?
Dot.
 Dot who?
Dot calm.

KNOCK-KNOCK!

What is the strongest part of a computer?
The Mighty Mouse.

What was the baby computer's first word?
"Goo-goo-google."

Why couldn't the computer find a good job?
It had no Internet connections.

How do you upgrade a computer?
Put it on a high shelf.

FUN FLASH!
Then there was the cyclops who just loved
his new eyePod.

SHELDON: I went to the computer store to buy the latest model, and the place was mobbed.

WELDON: Really? Did you have to wait online?

What is a dangerous computer?

It's one you have to enter at your own risk.

FUN FLASH!

Then there was the anti-social zombie who un-friended the undead.

What do you get when you cross the Internet and Harry Potter?

A computer wiz.

What do you call a trailer full of soft feathers?

A download.

FUN FLASH!

Spider-Man spends a lot of time working on his web page.

What's the fastest way to get in touch with Grandma?

Use Insta-grammy.

What happened when the clumsy guy dropped his computer?

He broke its windows.

What is the clothespin network?

It's an online service.

What is the hottest dating service online?

Matches.com.

What computer service does Santa use to look up Christmas information?

St. Nickapedia.

FUN FLASH!

Then there was the computer-tech circus clown who created a site called Funny Facebook.

Why was the computer sweating?

It was in a hot spot.

Knock-knock!
> Who's there?

Tweet he.
> Tweet he who?

Tweet-he-bird.

What game do young Internet fans like to play?
> Computer tech-tak-toe.

Knock-knock!
> Who's there?

I, Cher.
> I, Cher who?

I Cher like my new computer.

KNOCK-KNOCK!

FUN FLASHES!

Then there was the car computer that only made easy trips because he had no hard drive.

Then there was the dog named Bandit who loved his master's computer so much that he always slept on his laptop.

SHELDON: How is your job as a fantasy game developer?

WELDON: It's totally unreal!

Why did the computer shut down?

It was key bored.

Knock-knock!

Who's there?

Yukon.

Yukon who?

Yukon get online now.

5

SPORTY SNICKERS

What do you get when you cross a pastry chef and a hockey player?

A person who likes to ice the puck.

Why couldn't the golfer tee off?

His driver's license was revoked.

Knock-knock!
Who's there?
Hugo.
Hugo who?
Hugo long, and I'll throw you a pass.

FUN FLASH!

Then there was the ex-baseball player who made tons of money as a singer because he recorded a lot of catchy tunes.

Why did the baseball manager platoon Orville and Wilbur in the outfield?

Because they were both Wright fielders.

What's the best thing to have if a baseball stadium gets flooded?

A dugout canoe.

What did the leader of the Lumberjacks' Union yell to his workers?

"Tree strikes! We're out of here."

Knock-knock!

Who's there?

Flora Matz.

Flora Matz who?

Flora Matz are used in gymnastic competitions.

HA HA HA

Knock-knock!

Who's there?

Wrestle.

Wrestle who?

Wrestle a happy tune while you work.

What do you get when you cross a baseball thrower and an alien space craft?

A pitcher and a saucer.

Knock-knock!

Who's there?

Gnu.

Gnu who?

Gnu York Jets!

What do you call a mindless athletic contest performed on ice?

Go-figure skating.

What baseball position does the Abominable Snowman play?

Frost base.

What baseball position does a munchkin from Oz play?

Very short stop.

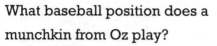

HA HA HA

---✂----------------------------------

WACKY WANT ADS

Wanted: Person needed to pack mittens in crates.
Object: Boxing gloves.

Wanted: Counterfeiter needed for game of catch
with football players.
Object: Passing the buck.

Wanted: Golfer with chauffeur's license to work for
florist.
Object: Driving Ms. Daisy.

Wanted: Gymnasts to work on parallel bars.
Object: Swing shifts.

Wanted: Boxer needed to regulate workplace hours.
Object: Punch-in-punch-out time clock.

What do you get when you cross a golfer and a gymnast?

A golf-cartwheel.

Where can you find a quarterback who is marooned on a tropical island?

In his hut, hut, hut!

SPORTS REPORTER: Was that your famous submarine pitch?
BASEBALL PITCHER: No, it was just an ordinary sinker.

FUN FLASH!

Dr. Frankenstein was a world-famous bodybuilder.

What did the heavyweight boxing champion do when he went to the pool?

He took a dive.

What did the offensive guard say to the nervous running back before the crucial fourth-down play?

"Don't worry! I'm pulling for you."

ED: Jed just jumped over the billiard table.

FRED: I guess that makes him a pool vaulter.

What did one bullpen pitcher say to the other bullpen pitcher?

"Quit steering at me."

KOOKY QUESTION

Do really tall basketball players like to be the center of attention?

What did the miserly hockey player wear on his feet?

Cheapskates.

LUKE: How was your golf game?

DUKE: It was awful. I kept hitting the ball off the fairway.

LUKE: Gee, that was a rough day at the course.

Why did the Munchkin baseball manager challenge the umpire's call?

He wanted to see it on wee-play.

Knock-knock!
> Who's there?

Juan.
> Juan who?

Juan a mile every day and you'll be in great shape.

When do you play baseball in the Mattress League?
> During spring training.

What is a pro wrestler's favorite time of year?
> The fall.

Why couldn't the Human Torch become a successful race car driver?
> He spent too much time burning rubber.

Why is a ninth-inning pitcher always the last person to leave the baseball locker room?
> Because he's the door closer.

Knock-knock!
> Who's there?

Dial us.
> Dial us who?

Dial-us Cowboys.

KNOCK-KNOCK!

What do you get when you cross a pro golfer and a plumber?

A guy who is great at sinking putts.

MEL: Did you hear about the softball player who quit sports to go into the music business?
NELL: No! Why did she do that?
MEL: She wanted to have a hit song.

What did one pro wrestler say to the other pro wrestler?

"Let's flip to see who wins this match."

KOOKY QUESTION
Do plumbers like to go toilet bowling?

What's big and furry and hangs out in an alley?
A bowler bear.

DON: Do you enjoy playing soccer?
JUAN: Yes! I get a kick out of it.

When the Jolly Green Giant pitches for the Jelly baseball team, does he ever throw bean balls?

Why wouldn't Marge let Bart play Little League baseball?

Because he kept trying to hit a homer.

Knock-knock!

Who's there?

Ooze.

Ooze who?

Ooze on first, What's on second, and I Don't Know is on third.

BABE: When do baseball fans get soaking wet?
ABE: When they get caught in a wave.

What is the sneakiest trick a gymnast can perform on the rings?

The iron double-cross.

Knock-knock!
    Who's there?
Jack Ease.
    Jack Ease who?
Jack Ease ride racehorses.

FUN FLASH!

Then there was the crooked soccer player who was banned from the sport for accepting kickbacks.

Knock-knock!
    Who's there?
Dewey.
    Dewey who?
Dewey have a chance for an upset?

Who won the first fish race?
    The catfish but only by a whisker.

Who won the bunny race?
    Jock Rabbit, by a hare.

DALE: Is it hard to be a pro motocross racer?
CALE: Yes. The life of a racer is a vicious cycle.

SILLY SPORTS NAMES

Beau N. Alley

Jim Nastics

Val E. Ball

Otto D. Park

Bat Minton

Grace Track

Bat R. Upp

KOOKY QUESTION

Do track-and-field high jumpers look forward to a leap year?

What do you get when you cross a mean hockey player and a prizefighter?

A penalty boxer.

What do you get when you cross a pigskin and an elephant?

A football the size of a hot-air balloon.

HA HA HA HA HA HA HA HA HA HA

FUN FLASH!

Then there was the Bee League baseball pitcher who got suspended for buzzing batters with his fast ball.

NUTTY B-BALL NAMES

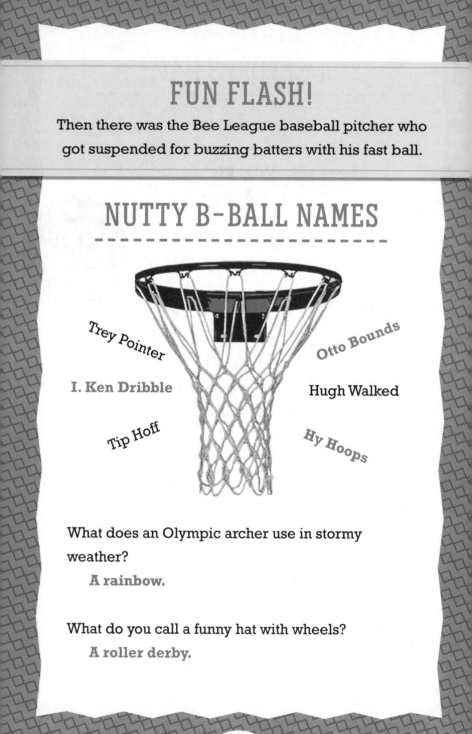

Trey Pointer

Otto Bounds

I. Ken Dribble

Hugh Walked

Tip Hoff

Hy Hoops

What does an Olympic archer use in stormy weather?

A rainbow.

What do you call a funny hat with wheels?

A roller derby.

FITNESS NAME FUN

HA HA HA HA

Cal Isthenics

X. Ercise

Ron N. Place

Sid Upps

Brenda Knees

Spin Glass

Yuhl Sweatalot

FUN FLASH!

Then there was the biker who became a baseball slugger and once hit for the motorcycle.

Where do hairdressers sit at the baseball stadium?
In the bleachers.

WACKY WORDS

"Grr! I'm a center, not a guard," the angry offensive lineman snapped.

HA HA HA HA

What do you get when you cross a mathematician and a home-plate umpire?

A person that counts batters out.

BUD: Why did you give up competitive surfing?
DUDE: I got surf bored.

ZACK: What's it like to be a big-league homerun hitter?
MACK: The job isn't what it's cracked up to be.

ZACK: How's your job as a professional tennis official?
MACK: It has its faults.

ZACK: What's it like to play pro basketball for a living?
MACK: The job has its ups and downs.

ZACK: What's it like to work as a NASCAR driver?
MACK: It's a rat race.

FUN FLASH!

Then there was the sheepherder who became an athlete and won a *baa*mitton championship.

BABE: On our ball team, we have a rabbi, a parson, a priest, a minister, and a reverend.
ABE: Isn't that a little strange?
BABE: Not really. They're all good baseball prayers.

Knock-knock!
Who's there?
Hindi.
Hindi who?
Hindi ninth inning, I hit a homerun to win the baseball game.

KNOCK-KNOCK!

What football position did the three-hundred-pound duck play?
He was a down lineman.

What do you call a baseball game between a chicken team and a duck team?
A fowl brawl.

LON: What's it like to be a professional baseball umpire?

DON: Sometimes I want to walk off the job and go on strike.

BILL: What's it like to be a pro volleyball player?

JILL: You can take my job and spike it.

What do you get when you cross a New York football team and a very large vegetable farmer?

The New York Jolly Green Giants.

FUNNY FOOTBALL ROSTER

Q. B. Sachs

Wade Receiver

T. D. Kech

Dee Scenter

Paul N. Guard

Furs Down

Ed Coach

Walter Buoy

Mike A. Tackle

D. Bach

Red Zone

What did the duck quarterback say to his teammates?

"Let's puddle up!"

NICK: Hey, dude! What is a superhero's favorite golf club?

RICK: It's a four iron, man!

Which baseball squad has the team motto "Always be prepared"?

The Chicago Cub Scouts.

What do you get when you cross a pro basketball team and a dairy farm?

The Cleveland Calves.

What do you get when you cross a Wisconsin football team and a TV show about antique archaeology?

The Green Bay Pickers.

Knock-knock!

Who's there?

A Sam Boney.

A Sam Boney who?

A Sam Boney is a machine
that resurfaces the ice in
a hockey rink.

What happens to a convict
pitcher if he cheats in a
baseball game?

He winds up in jail.

HA HA HA HA HA HA HA HA HA HA HA HA HA HA HA HA HA HA HA

6

What's the best
way to hit an Italian meatball?
Use a mozzarella stick.

Why did the potato
delivery truck slow down?
There was a dip in
the road.

How do you prepare roast
rooster?
You cook-a-doodle-do.

Knock-knock!

Who's there?

Ron Old.

Ron Old who?

Ron Old McDonald had a farm
and a fast-food restaurant.

What do you do with a smart hamburger?

You put it on the honor roll.

Where does the Jolly Green Burger King sleep?

On a bed of lettuce.

Who is the father of all bathrooms?

Papa John.

Knock-knock!

Who's there?

Menu.

Menu who?

Menu want to order, call a waiter
to your table.

What do sanitation workers like to eat for lunch?

Junk food.

KNOCK-KNOCK!

What do you get when you cross a famous pirate actor and a fast-food restaurant?

Johnny Depp Fried Chicken.

Where do football players order pizzas to-go?

At Pizza Hut, Hut, Hut!

Knock-knock!

Who's there?

Wendy.

Wendy who?

Wendy burgers are done,
put the hot dogs on the grill.

What kind of bread is very inquisitive?

Why bread.

FUNNY FOOD FLASH!

Then there was the munchkin who worked in the Oz Diner as a short-order cook.

Who are Peter, Marsha, and Cindy Grape?

They're members of the Brady Bunch.

Do fortune-tellers order their steaks
cooked medium?

Knock-knock!
> Who's there?

Heidi.
> Heidi who?

Heidi candy! Mom and Dad are off their diets.

Where was the first Burger King found?
> In a royal food court.

Who did the salad dressing vote for?
> Mayor Naise.

What kind of meat does a martial arts expert like?
> Karate chops.

What did one grape say to the other grape?
> "I'm vine today. How are you?"

SLIM: What is a golfer's favorite breakfast meat?
JIM: Sausage links.

Where does the Jolly Green Giant keep his baby niblets?

In corn cribs.

SKYLER: Why does relish giggle so much?
TYLER: It's pickle-ish.

Knock-knock!

Who's there?

Burgers.

Burgers who?

Burgers can't be choosers.

What is the specialty of the Caveman's Deli?

A club sandwich.

CUSTOMER: Hey, waiter! Why is my hamburger squashed flat?
WAITER: Well, sir, you said you wanted a cola and a burger and to step on it.

What kind of Mexican food do you find on the beach?

Taco shells.

What do you get when you cross a thoroughbred and a vegetable?

Horseradish.

LUKE: How does Popeye deep-fry fish?
DUKE: He uses Olive Oil.

Knock-knock!

Who's there?

Sizzle.

Sizzle who?

Sizzle be the last time I eat in this crummy cafeteria.

What do you find in a fountain at a dance school?

Tap water.

LENNY: What are a taxidermist's favorite veggies?
DENNY: Stuffed peppers and stuffed cabbage.

What is a hamburger baseball contest?

It's a game of ketchup.

Who did the Burger King fall in love with?

The Dairy Queen.

Why did the hungry teen go to a fast-food restaurant?

Because he had a Hardee appetite.

Why didn't the golfer go into the fast-food restaurant?

He pulled up to the drive-through window instead.

What happens when a banana gets sunburnt?

It starts to peel.

Knock-knock!

Who's there?

Turnip.

Turnip who?

Turnip the TV; this is my favorite cooking show.

KNOCK-KNOCK!

What did the waitress ask Spider-Man when he ordered a burger?

Do you want flies with that?

FUN FOOD FLASH!

Then there was the hungry jeweler who went to a fast-food restaurant and ordered onion rings.

What do you get when you cross hay fever and ground beef?

Sneezeburgers.

What do you call a spoiled sausage link?

Bratwurst.

Knock-knock!

Who's there?

Liver.

Liver who?

Liver alone. She doesn't like to be bothered during lunch.

HA HA HA

RHYME TIME

Jack was hungry.
Jack was quick.
Jack ate fast,
And now he's sick.

What happened to the clumsy acrobatic hot dogs?

They fell on their buns.

When does a snacker scrape the bottom of the barrel?

When the chips are down.

BILLY: Did you fix our dinner?

LILLY: I tried to fix it, but it still tastes awful.

What did the slice of bread say to the margarine?

"Now that you've buttered me up, what do you really want?"

ROB: I flunked out of cooking school.

BOB: How did you do that?

ROB: I failed all the taste tests.

What do you call a worried hot dog?

A frankfretter.

How did the beaver get splinters in its tongue?

It ate some wooden table scraps.

Knock-knock!

Who's there?

Preppy.

Preppy who?

Preppy-roni pizza sure tastes good.

JUDY: What do birdbrains like to eat for a snack?

TRUDY: I don't know, what?

JUDY: Chocolate-chirp cookies.

TRUDY: How do you make chocolate-chirp cookies?

JUDY: I'll tweet you the recipe.

FUN FOOD FLASH!

Then there was the baseball umpire who missed his mom's cooking so much that he dreamed of eating off home plate.

What's the worst kind of cake you can eat?

A cake of soap.

What's red and swims in the ocean?

A strawberry jellyfish.

What did the sheepherder have for lunch?

A *baa*loney sandwich.

What kind of steak does Peter cook in Neverland?

Pan-fried steak.

SKYLER: What do you like best about my sponge cake?
TYLER: It's very moist.

Why was the bread dough so sad?
It wanted to be kneaded by someone.

What is the favorite soft drink of pastry chefs?
Baking soda.

What did the hungry prince of England have for lunch?
A Buckingham sandwich.

What does the Gingerbread Boy have on his bed?
A cookie sheet.

What do you get when you cross a handstand and a menu?
A balanced diet.

What patriotic vegetable said, "I regret that I have but one life to give for my country"?
Nathan Kale.

HA HA HA

THE ABOMINABLE SNOWMAN'S GROCERY LIST

Frozen Yogurt
Cold Cuts
Iced Tea
Chili Beans
Snow Peas
Italian Ice
Kool-Aid

Knock-knock!
>   **Who's there?**
A belly.
>   **A belly who?**
A belly doughnut is sweet to eat.

KNOCK-KNOCK!

What do you get if you eat tangled string cheese?
>   **A knot in your stomach.**

What should you do if the front door of a Mexican restaurant is locked?
>   **Ring the Taco Bell.**

FUN FOOD FLASH!

Then there was the tuna fisherman who showed up late for work and got canned on the spot.

Knock-knock!
> Who's there?

Lettuce.
> Lettuce who?

Lettuce alone, we're busy.

CHEF: How do you make giggle soup?
COOK: Use laughingstock.

What's green and yellow and has four wheels and a meter?
> A taxi cabbage.

What did the miner put in his black coffee?
> Coal cream.

What does a beaver's diet consist of?
> Tree square meals a day.

HA HA HA
HA HA HA

Knock-knock!

Who's there?

Dill.

Dill who?

Dill death do us part.

Why did the motorist put raw vegetables in his empty tank?

Because raw vegetables give you plenty of gas.

GOOFY GROCERY STAFF

Mr. Lettuce—he's the head man.

Ms. Carrot—she cooks up hare-brained marketing concepts.

Mr. Corn—he's always popping off.

Mr. Chili Pepper—he's hot-tempered.

Ms. Sugar Beet—she's very sweet.

What did the little bunny order at the fast-food restaurant?

A hoppy meal.

FUNNY FOOD NAMES

Mr. Bill Loney

Mr. Sal Ammie

Ms. Liv R. Wurst

Mr. Caesar Sal Add

Mr. Mack A. Roney

Miss Barbie Que

Mr. Lem Chops

Mr. Chuck Stake

Miss Bebe Food

Mr. Porter House

Mr. Frank Furter

Miss Angel Kake

Miss Em Full

What is the motto of a southern-fried chicken chef?

"If at first you don't succeed, fry, fry again."

MATT: Why don't you ever eat lunch at the tennis club?
PAT: The waiters do a bad job of serving.

How do you make a hula hamburger?

You order a burger and shake.

Which New York City baseball team do Wendy and Ronald root for?

The New York Meats.

Knock-knock!

Who's there?

Cyrano.

Cyrano who?

Cyrano how to cook a hamburger.

KNOCK-KNOCK!

KOOKY QUESTION

Do corporate bees gather for a buzzness lunch?

Where did the prizefighter eat his lunch?

At a fist-food restaurant.

HA HA HA
HA HA HA HA HA

7

ROCK 'N' RIDDLES

What do you get when you cross a trendy female singing star and a baby?

Lady Ga-ga-goo-goo.

What is the favorite old rock band of zombies?

The Grateful Undead.

What kind of rock music do prospectors love?

Solid golden oldies.

ROCK NEWS FLASH!

Then there was the tall basketball player who quit
the NBA to become the lead singer of a band.
Now he's a front-and-center man.

What did the drum say to the bass guitar?
"Don't try to beat me up."

Knock-knock!
Who's there?
K. T.
K. T. who?
K. T. Perry.

ROCK NEWS FLASH!

The Tin Man is a metalhead.

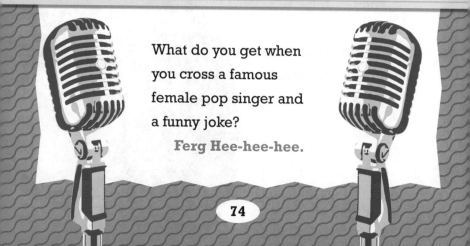

What do you get when
you cross a famous
female pop singer and
a funny joke?
Ferg Hee-hee-hee.

What kind of music do Grandma and Grandpa listen to?

Old folk music.

What is the Jolly Green Giant's favorite music group?

The Black Eyed Peas.

How does the rock musician dig a hole?

He uses a guitar pick.

Knock-knock!

Who's there?

Adele.

Adele who?

Adele performance makes for a boring concert.

ROCK STAR FLASH!

The Black Eyed Peas and iPods are a perfect match.

Knock-knock!

Who's there?

Evan Lee.

Evan Lee who?

Evan Lee music is gospel music.

What do you call a rabbit rapper?

A hip-hoppity artist.

HA HA HA

What do you get when you cross a reality TV show for aspiring singers and an audio echo device?

The Voice, Voice, Voice, Voice. . . .

What do you get when you cross a tornado and a popular band?

A whirl tour.

Which instrument does the Rockin' Jolly Green Giant play?

The Pea-ano.

KOOKY QUESTION

Could MC Hammer and Nine Inch Nails put together a hit album?

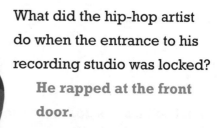

What did the hip-hop artist do when the entrance to his recording studio was locked?

He rapped at the front door.

What do you get when you cross a band and a small computer?

A musical notebook.

Why did the singing cow move to New York City?

She wanted to be in a Broadway *moosical*.

What would you get if Picasso were a good singer?

A recording artist.

What is the Ghostbusters' favorite kind of music?

Rhythm and boos.

What do you get when you cross a female superstar singer and the movie *Jaws*?

Sharkira.

What is the favorite music of Demolition Derby drivers?

Wreck 'n' Roll.

Knock-knock!

Who's there?

Sheena.

Sheena who?

Sheena guitar pick around here?

KNOCK-
KNOCK!

Which music group does Charlie Brown listen to on Halloween?

The Smashing Great Pumpkins.

Knock-knock!

Who's there?

Roy Al.

Roy Al who?

Roy Al rockers include Sir Paul McCartney and Sir Mick Jagger.

What kind of classic rock is green and fuzzy?

Moldy Oldies.

Knock-knock!

Who's there?

Sheik.

Sheik who?

Sheik it up, baby!

KNOCK-KNOCK!

Where are the hottest rock tunes stored?

In the Rock and Roll Hall of Flame.

Who is Bilbo's and Frodo's favorite rock star?

Elvish Presley.

What do you get when you cross an easy-open bottle top and a loud yell?

Twist and shout.

SILLY SINGING STARS

Harvey Metal

B. A. Singer

Ann Core

Rock N. Band

Goldie Oldie

Gus Poole

Rock Dee House

Todd Lars Tunes

Which popular female singer is also a fashion designer?

Tailor Swift.

Knock-knock!

Who's there?

Ann Dee.

Ann Dee who?

Ann Dee Grammer is a pop star.

Which female pop singer has a swarm of faithful fans?

Bee-yoncé.

What do you get when you cross a famous country singer and a librarian?

Garth Books.

What rock star has pine needles and is nicknamed "The Boss"?

Spruce Springsteen.

Why did the rock band give a concert while standing in a creek?

Because they wanted to stream live music.

What do you get when you cross a mattress and fast music?

Soft rock.

What did Ringo do after the Beatles broke up?

He tried to drum up some business for himself.

What did Mother Nature do at the outdoor concert?

She danced up a storm.

Show me a famous rock band holding oars . . . and I'll show you the Rowing Stones.

Knock-knock!

Who's there?

Al Blums.

Al Blums who?

Al Blums take a long time to record.

Knock-knock!

Who's there?

Khan.

Khan who?

Khan-certs are fun to go to.

KNOCK-KNOCK!

What do you call a roar of approval at a concert?

A rockin' cheer.

What is jelly music?

Songs recorded during a jam session.

Why did the Watchmen's band sound so bad?

All the musicians were out of time.

How do you pay an audio expert?

Give him a sound check.

Knock-knock!

Who's there?

Piccolo.

Piccolo who?

Piccolo number when you play the lottery.

What do you get when you cross band teachers and math teachers?

Musicians who know a lot of musical numbers.

What kind of vehicle never knows the words to any songs?

A Hummer.

8

WISE CRACKERS

Matt: Hi, Lemon Head.

PAT: What a childish thing to say. How old are you anyway?

MATT: Old enough to know bitter.

ZACK: My family is in the steel business.

MACK: So, you're nothing but a bunch of thieves?

MILLIE: Why did you give me that dirty look?

TILLIE: Because your face needs washing.

ZELDA: My boyfriend isn't a fast thinker.

NELDA: That's for sure. He's definitely a snail male.

ARTIE: What's your frank opinion of me?

MARTY: You're a big wiener!

ZINGERS!

The only time you have something on your mind is when you wear a hat!

Your IQ is so low, it's measured in negative numbers!

You're such a blockhead that instead of dandruff, you get sawdust!

Join the fight against air pollution! Please take a shower every day.

NICK: I can't think straight anymore.

RICK: That's because you're all bent out of shape.

NELL: I never say anything bad about anyone else.

MEL: That's only because you're always talking about yourself.

BEN: Ouch! I have a splinter in my finger.

JEN: How did you get it? Scratching your head?

TED: I have a smartphone.

ED: It's too bad your phone can't say the same thing about its owner.

HA
HA HA

9

DON'T GET SMART

Gordon: Why didn't you like that special bye-ology class?

MORGAN: Because it was so long.

How does an acrobat read a textbook?

She flips through the pages.

What do you put at the end of a cafeteria sentence?

A lunch period.

Knock-knock!

Who's there?

Venice.

Venice who?

Venice the last day of school?

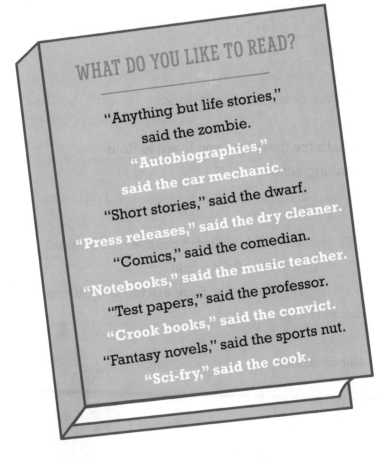

WHAT DO YOU LIKE TO READ?

"Anything but life stories," said the zombie.

"Autobiographies," said the car mechanic.

"Short stories," said the dwarf.

"Press releases," said the dry cleaner.

"Comics," said the comedian.

"Notebooks," said the music teacher.

"Test papers," said the professor.

"Crook books," said the convict.

"Fantasy novels," said the sports nut.

"Sci-fry," said the cook.

Why did the girl bring her cell phone to the cafeteria?

Because she wanted to have a tweet after lunch.

What do band students sit on during class?

Musical chairs.

Knock-knock!

Who's there?

Avenue.

Avenue who?

Avenue done your homework?

What's the first thing you learn to do in banking school?

Check attendance.

STUDENT: I did this math problem five times.
TEACHER: Excellent work!
STUDENT: Not really. Here are the five different answers I got.

Knock-knock!

Who's there?

Holt.

Holt who?

Holt the door open. This is a fire drill.

What has numbered pages and works for a news service?

A book reporter.

Why are elephants so smart?

They never forget their lessons.

TEACHER: Our president is married to the First Lady.
STUDENT: My bible-school teacher said Adam was married to the first lady.

Knock-knock!

Who's there?

Sheila.

Sheila who?

Shelia be late for class if she doesn't hurry.

FUN FLASH!

When the Tin Man of Oz was a tween,
he went to metal school.

What did the encyclopedia say to the naked textbook?

"**Cover yourself.**"

TEACHER: Your daughter is a good student, but she has trouble making up her mind. Can you explain why that is?
MOTHER: Well . . . yes and no.

Show me a class in mannequin construction . . . and I'll show you some test dummies.

What did the math teacher do when she had too many students?

She divided the class.

PRINCIPAL: How did all these cafeteria plates get smashed?
TEACHER'S AIDE: Lunch breaks.

SIGN IN A FINISHING SCHOOL CAFETERIA
Only students with good taste eat here.

Knock-knock!

> Who's there?

I, Mustard.

> I, Mustard who?

I Mustard lost my homework.

TED: I like to read history books. Do you?
FRED: No. It's just old news.

CRAZY QUESTION!

The dental school quiz format:
Answer true or false teeth.

The banking school quiz format:
Fill in the blank checks.

The bible school quiz format:
Yes or Noah answers.

Why couldn't little Mickey use his computer in school?

He left his Minnie Mouse at home.

Knock-knock!

Who's there?

Don Pyle.

Don Pyle who?

Don Pyle on the homework tonight.

GUY: Why did Abe Lincoln write the Gettysburg Address?

SKY: He didn't have a computer and there was no e-mail.

GAL: Why didn't you do well in barber school?

AL: I took too many shortcuts.

HA HA HA HA HA HA HA HA HA HA HA HA

FUN FLASH!

Then there was the track star who wanted to go to law school, so he ran for student council.

ZACK: How did you become the class clown?
MACK: Funny you should ask. I don't know. I guess the joke is on me.

Knock-knock!
    Who's there?
Warren.
    Warren who?
Warren you in my class last year?

Why did the lunch lady go to the optometrist?
    She kept seeing double cheeseburgers.

SIGN IN A DRIVERS' EDUCATION CLASS
This course is wheel fun!

Why did the clock have to stay after school?
    It wouldn't stop tick-tocking during class.

FUN FLASH!

Then there was the painter who went to flight school and passed his pilot's test with flying colors.

MARTY: I studied all night for today's exam.

ARTIE: So what happened?

MARTY: I fell asleep during the test.

Knock-knock!

> Who's there?

It's Tory.

> It's Tory who?

It's Tory time. Read us a book.

KNOCK-KNOCK!

Knock-knock!

> Who's there?

I taught.

> I taught who?

I taught I taw a puddy tat!

MATT: I went to baseball school to learn how to steal bases.

PAT: How did you do?

MATT: I got thrown out.

PENNY: I took a class on how to balance a budget.

JENNY: And so what happened?

PENNY: I made a clumsy attempt to pass, but ended up dropping the course.

KOOKY QUESTION

Can students at the School for Mutants earn X-tra credit?

TEACHER: Melanie, you get an A. Nick, you get a B.

MARTY: Hey, teacher. What about me?

TEACHER: Marty, I'll C you later.

Who does little Thor go to see if he falls down during recess?

The school Norse.

MEL: I took a course on student loans.

DELL: What happened?

MEL: I got no credit.

Knock-knock!

Who's there?

I. M. Irving.

I. M. Irving who?

I. M. Irving a hard time with my algebra problems.

KNOCK-KNOCK!

Knock-knock!

Who's there?

I'm Gladys.

I'm Gladys who?

I'm Gladys class is over.

Knock-knock!

Who's there?

Velma.

Velma who?

Velma work is done. Now I can go home.